★ THE ★
UNITED
STATES
PRESIDENTS

JIMMY CARTER

Heidi M.D. Elston

Checkerboard Library

An Imprint of Abdo Publishing
abdobooks.com

ABDOBOOKS.COM

Published by Abdo Publishing, a division of ABDO, PO Box 398166, Minneapolis, Minnesota 55439. Copyright © 2021 by Abdo Consulting Group, Inc. International copyrights reserved in all countries. No part of this book may be reproduced in any form without written permission from the publisher. Checkerboard Library™ is a trademark and logo of Abdo Publishing.

Printed in the United States of America, North Mankato, Minnesota
052020
092020

Design: Emily O'Malley, Kelly Doudna, Mighty Media, Inc.
Production: Mighty Media, Inc.
Editor: Liz Salzmann

Cover Photograph: Getty Images
Interior Photographs: Albert de Bruijn/iStockphoto, p. 37; AP Images, pp. 6, 17, 23, 36; Carol M. Highsmith/Library of Congress, p. 32; The Carter Center, p. 31; Courtesy: Jimmy Carter Library, pp. 6 (wedding), 7, 12, 13, 16, 25, 29; Dirck Halstead/Getty Images, p. 27; Getty Images, pp. 11, 15, 19, 22; John Amis/AP Images, p. 33; Karl Schumacher/Getty Images, p. 5; Library of Congress, pp. 7 (Reagan), 21, 40; National Park Service, p. 10; Pete Souza/Flickr, p. 44; Shutterstock Images, pp. 6 (Plains sign, statue), 7 (Carter Center), 38, 39; Warren K. Leffler/Library of Congress, p. 24; Wikimedia Commons, pp. 40 (George Washington), 42

Library of Congress Control Number: 2019956436

Publisher's Cataloging-in-Publication Data
Names: Elston, Heidi M.D., author.
Title: Jimmy Carter / by Heidi M.D. Elston
Description: Minneapolis, Minnesota : Abdo Publishing, 2021 | Series: The United States presidents | Includes online resources and index.
Identifiers: ISBN 9781532193439 (lib. bdg.) | ISBN 9781098212070 (ebook)
Subjects: LCSH: Carter, Jimmy, 1924---Juvenile literature. | Presidents--Biography--Juvenile literature. | Presidents--United States--History--Juvenile literature. | Legislators--United States --Biography--Juvenile literature. | Politics and government--Biography--Juvenile literature.
Classification: DDC 973.926092--dc23

★ CONTENTS ★

Jimmy Carter

In November 1976, Jimmy Carter was elected the thirty-ninth US president. Because of recent government **scandals**, many Americans were looking for a change. Carter's main goal was to return honor and pride to the president's office.

Carter emphasized morality in government. He also believed the government should help the poor and the needy. Voters trusted Carter and felt comfortable with him. He was a simple man from a small farm town in the Deep South.

At the time Carter became president, the US **economy** was in trouble. Prices of food, gas, and many other items people needed to live were rising. Buying a house was hard, and saving for the future was even harder.

As his presidency was nearing a close, Carter ran for reelection. But many people blamed him for the country's economic problems. So, he lost the election.

Today, Carter continues to give back to his country. He remains an image of honor and pride in America.

★ TIMELINE ★

1946

Carter graduated from the US Naval Academy in Annapolis, Maryland. On July 7, he married Eleanor Rosalynn Smith.

1963

On January 14, Carter took office as a Georgia state senator.

1977

Carter took office as the thirty-ninth US president on January 20. Carter asked Congress to pass the Emergency Natural Gas Act.

1924

On October 1, James Earl Carter Jr. was born in Plains, Georgia.

1953

Carter quit the navy.

1970

Carter was elected governor of Georgia.

1964

Carter was reelected to the Georgia state senate.

1974

On December 12, Carter announced his candidacy for president.

1978

Carter made history by arranging a meeting between Israeli prime minister Menachem Begin and Egyptian president Anwar Sadat. The US Senate approved two treaties regarding the Panama Canal.

1982

Mr. and Mrs. Carter founded the Carter Center in Atlanta, Georgia.

1986

The Carter Presidential Center complex was dedicated.

1979

On November 4, more than 50 Americans were taken hostage in Iran.

1980

Carter lost his bid for reelection to Ronald Reagan.

2002

Carter received the Nobel Peace Prize.

1999

Mr. and Mrs. Carter each received the Presidential Medal of Freedom.

“ I say to you quite frankly that

the time for racial discrimination is over.”

DID YOU KNOW?

★ From a young age, Carter knew he wanted to join the navy. He thought his feet were flat and worried the US Naval Academy wouldn't accept him. So, he rolled his feet over Coke bottles to strengthen his arches.

★ Carter was a speed-reader. He could read 2,000 words per minute!

★ Carter was the first US Naval Academy graduate to become a US president.

★ Carter was the first president to walk with his family from his inauguration ceremony at the US Capitol to the White House.

★ Carter is the longest-living US president.

Little Jimmy

James Earl Carter Jr. was born on October 1, 1924, in Plains, Georgia. He was called Jimmy. Jimmy was the oldest son of James Earl Carter Sr. and Lillian Gordy Carter. He had two sisters, Gloria and Ruth. His brother was named William. The family called him Billy.

Lillian Gordy Carter and James Earl Carter Sr.

Jimmy's father was called Earl. Earl was a farmer and a businessman. He grew corn, cotton, and peanuts. Earl also operated a small general store in Archery, Georgia.

Lillian, Jimmy's mother, was a registered nurse. She was a caring, giving woman. Often, she helped patients without receiving any pay. Lillian also loved to read books and travel.

The Carter family moved to Archery when Jimmy was four. There, they lived in a small house

When Jimmy was young, Plains was a small town. About 600 people lived there.

without plumbing or electricity. They were members of the Plains Baptist Church. Religion, education, and hard work were important to the family.

Jimmy began his business career at a young age. When he was only five, he began selling boiled peanuts. On weekdays, Jimmy earned one dollar a day. He made about five dollars on Saturdays!

A Dream Fulfilled

Jimmy attended public schools in nearby Plains. He was a good student. His favorite subjects were history, literature, and music. And like his mother, Jimmy loved to read. He even belonged to a book lovers' club. Jimmy graduated high school at the top of his class. He was the first member of his family to graduate from high school.

In 1941, Jimmy attended Georgia Southwestern College in Americus. The next year, he entered the Georgia Institute of Technology in Atlanta.

Jimmy fulfilled a childhood dream in 1943. That year, he entered the US Naval Academy in Annapolis, Maryland. Jimmy was an excellent student. He

Jimmy's first naval assignment was on the USS *Wyoming* out of Norfolk, Virginia.

liked military studies and training. In 1946, Jimmy graduated fifty-ninth in a class of 820.

The year before his graduation, Jimmy had started dating his sister Ruth's best friend. Eleanor Rosalynn Smith, known as Rosalynn, was also from Plains. Jimmy married Rosalynn on July 7, 1946.

Jimmy spent more than six years as a naval officer. In 1948, he was accepted for submarine duty. Jimmy quickly moved up the ranks. His naval career seemed promising. Then tragedy struck, and Jimmy's plans changed instantly.

Mr. and Mrs. Carter were married at Plains Methodist Church.

Family Man

In 1953, James Earl Carter Sr. died. At that time, he was a member of the Georgia House of Representatives. People throughout the state were saddened by his death.

Carter saw how his father had touched people's lives. He decided he wanted to model his life after his father's. So, Carter quit the navy later that year. Then, he returned to Plains.

In Plains, Carter worked hard to make the family farm and peanut business successful. He also became involved in local government. Carter served on the school board. He was also a member of the library and hospital boards.

Carter tried to **integrate** schools and churches in the area. But many of his neighbors did not agree with his views on racial issues. So, Carter's efforts failed.

By this time, the Carters had three sons. John William "Jack" had been born in 1947. James Earl III "Chip" followed in 1950. And, Donnel Jeffrey "Jeff" had been born in 1952. The Carters had their daughter, Amy Lynn, in 1967.

Mr. and Mrs. Carter (*center*) with their extended family

Stopping Voter Fraud

In 1962, Carter sought the **Democratic** nomination for the Georgia state senate. He lost the **primary** election to Homer Moore by just 139 votes. Carter believed Moore had won because of **fraud**. So, he fought the election results and requested the votes be recounted.

After the recount, Carter was declared the winner of the primary. He had just three days to prepare for the general election! Still, Carter won by about 1,000 votes.

On January 14, 1963, Carter took office. As a state senator, he oversaw the budget and did not waste money. Carter also promoted programs that helped the poor. And, he fought for education reforms. People loved his ideas. They reelected Carter to the Georgia state senate in 1964.

JIMMY CARTER
FOR STATE SENATOR

Carter's senate campaign poster

Carter (*fourth from left*) being sworn into the Georgia state senate

Governor Carter

In 1966, Carter announced he would run for governor of Georgia. However, he did not win the **Democratic** nomination. Carter wasn't discouraged. Right away, he made plans to run again in four years.

Carter was elected governor of Georgia in 1970. His term began the next year on January 12. Carter was different from most southern governors at that time. He supported **integration**. And, he appointed many African Americans to state government jobs.

As governor, Carter made a series of reforms. One reform provided equal state aid to schools in wealthy and poor areas. Carter also passed laws to protect the **environment**.

Governor Carter traveled often. He also welcomed many international visitors. And, he met with leading national politicians. Carter believed he would make an able president. So, on December 12, 1974, Carter announced he would run for president.

Lillian Carter recalled learning of her son's desire to run for president in 1973. He told her, "Momma, I'm going to run for president of the United States, and I'm going to win."

Watergate Scandal

Meanwhile, a political **scandal** called Watergate had rocked the country. Americans were left with a distrust for their government. The scandal is named after the Watergate office **complex** in Washington, DC.

There, police arrested five men on June 17, 1972. The men had broken into the **Democratic National Committee** headquarters. They were there to steal secrets to help **Republican** president Richard Nixon's reelection campaign.

About 40 people were charged with crimes in relation to the scandal. These included several top White House aides. For months, President Nixon denied involvement in the break-in and the cover-up that followed. Yet on August 9, 1974, he resigned.

That day, Vice President Gerald Ford became the thirty-eighth US president. He stated, "Our long national nightmare is over." One month later, Ford pardoned Nixon. This meant that any crimes Nixon may have committed were forgiven. As a result, Ford's popularity dropped. This would help Carter in the next presidential election.

Nixon defended himself during the Watergate

The 1976 Election

The 1976 **Democratic National Convention** was held in New York City, New York. There, party leaders chose Carter as their candidate for president. US senator Walter Mondale was named his **running mate**. The **Republican** Party nominated President Ford. He chose Senator Bob Dole as his running mate.

Carter's "Peanut Brigade" was a group of friends and other volunteers who campaigned for him.

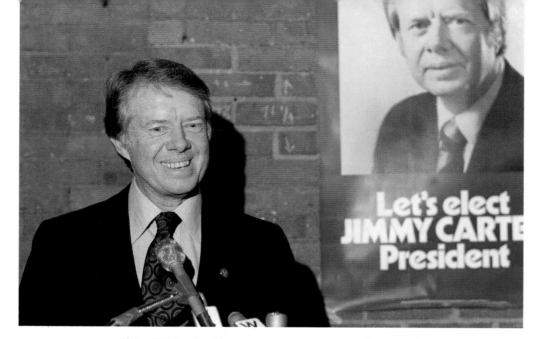

The 1976 election was very close. It wasn't until 3:30 a.m. that Carter knew he had won.

Carter was not well-known. But he appealed to many different kinds of people. Carter campaigned as an honest and trustworthy man. He pledged to create more jobs. He also promised to reorganize the federal government. Many men had avoided the **draft** during the **Vietnam War**. Carter declared he would consider granting pardons to them.

The 1976 election for president was the closest in more than 60 years. On November 2, Carter won a narrow victory. He earned 297 electoral votes, while Ford received 240 votes.

Running the Country

On January 20, 1977, Carter was **inaugurated** as the thirty-ninth US president. One of Carter's first acts as president fulfilled a campaign promise. He pardoned those who had avoided the **draft** during the **Vietnam War**.

Carter took office during one of the worst winters in US history. Because the weather was so cold, people used a lot of natural gas for heat. This caused a natural gas shortage. So, Carter asked Congress to pass the Emergency Natural Gas Act. This plan sent natural gas to areas of the country with severe shortages.

Another concern was the US **economy**. Many Americans were without jobs. And prices for food, clothes, houses, and other basic necessities were high. President Carter focused on improving the economy. But expenses continued to increase. As a result, Carter's popularity fell.

An oil crisis in 1979 led to a shortage of gasoline. People waited in long lines to buy gas.

Joan and Walter Mondale with Rosalynn and Jimmy Carter

PRESIDENT CARTER'S CABINET

ONE TERM
January 20, 1977–January 20, 1981

- ★ **STATE:** Cyrus Vance
  Edmund S. Muskie (from May 8, 1980)

- ★ **TREASURY:** W. Michael Blumenthal
  George W. Miller (from August 6, 1979)

- ★ **DEFENSE:** Harold Brown

- ★ **ATTORNEY GENERAL:** Griffin B. Bell
  Benjamin R. Civiletti (from August 16, 1979)

- ★ **INTERIOR:** Cecil Dale Andrus

- ★ **AGRICULTURE:** Robert S. Bergland

- ★ **COMMERCE:** Juanita M. Kreps
  Philip M. Klutznick (from January 9, 1980)

- ★ **LABOR:** F. Ray Marshall

- ★ **HEALTH, EDUCATION, AND WELFARE:** Joseph A. Califano Jr.
  Patricia Roberts Harris (from August 3, 1979)

- ★ **HEALTH AND HUMAN SERVICES:** Patricia Roberts Harris
  (from September 27, 1979)

- ★ **HOUSING AND URBAN DEVELOPMENT:** Patricia Roberts Harris
  Moon Landrieu (from September 24, 1979)

- ★ **TRANSPORTATION:** Brock Adams
  Neil E. Goldschmidt (from September 24, 1979)

- ★ **ENERGY:** James R. Schlesinger (from October 1, 1977)
  Charles W. Duncan Jr. (from August 24, 1979)

- ★ **EDUCATION:** Shirley M. Hufstedler (from December 6, 1979)

President Jimmy Carter

Foreign Affairs

President Carter had better success helping other countries. He participated in **summit** meetings in Europe and Japan. He also traveled to South America, Africa, Asia, and the Middle East. There, he promoted world peace.

In 1978, President Carter made history. He conducted a meeting between Israeli prime minister Menachem Begin and Egyptian president Anwar Sadat. The two leaders agreed to create a peace treaty. Egypt and Israel adopted the treaty the following year.

Also in 1978, the US Senate approved two treaties related to the **Panama Canal**. The United States had controlled the canal since the early 1900s. One treaty granted control of the canal to Panama by the year 2000. The second treaty allowed the United States to defend the canal's **neutrality**.

Then trouble struck. On November 4, 1979, the US **embassy** in Iran was seized. More than 50 Americans were taken as **hostages**. Carter tried to arrange their release. However, they were not freed until moments after Carter left office in 1981.

On March 26, 1979, Sadat (*left*), Carter, and Begin (*right*) celebrated the signing of the peace treaty between Egypt and Israel.

Problems with Iran and the US **economy** hurt Carter's chances for reelection. In November 1980, **Republican** Ronald Reagan defeated Carter. Carter received just 49 electoral votes. Reagan won 489.

A True Leader

After leaving the White House, Carter returned to Plains. He has remained active in retirement. Carter served as a professor at Emory University in Atlanta, Georgia. He also wrote more than 30 books.

Mr. and Mrs. Carter founded the Carter Center in 1982. It is based in Atlanta. The center works to resolve conflict throughout the world. It also fights disease, poverty, and hunger.

In 1986, the Carter Presidential Center **complex** was **dedicated**. Located in Atlanta, it includes the Carter Center and the Jimmy Carter Library and Museum.

The National Park Service manages the Jimmy Carter National Historic Site. It is located in Plains. The site is open to those interested in learning more about the former president.

Carter still travels to many countries. He promotes world peace and helps solve world problems. He also does much volunteer work. One week each year, Carter and his wife help with Habitat for Humanity. This organization helps needy people build homes for themselves. Carter

Carter often traveled around the world to promote good health.

also teaches Sunday school at the Maranatha Baptist Church in Plains.

In 1999, Mr. and Mrs. Carter each received the Presidential Medal of Freedom. This is the nation's highest honor for nonmilitary people. Then in 2002, Carter received the Nobel Peace Prize. Each year, this prize is awarded to a person who works for world peace.

Carter worked hard for many years and accomplished much. He had an excellent career in the US Navy and he

Mr. and Mrs. Carter continue their commitment to an improved quality of life worldwide.

Carter is devoted to human
rights and world peace.

turned a small peanut farm into a successful business.
Then he went on to a career in politics as a state senator,
governor, and US president.

Carter always did things the right way. He worked
honestly and never took shortcuts. From naval officer to
president, he truly led by example. Today, Jimmy Carter
remains a leader. Through volunteer work, he continues to
promote a better world for all people.

BRANCHES OF GOVERNMENT

The US government is divided into three branches. They are the executive, legislative, and judicial branches. This division is called a separation of powers. Each branch has some power over the others. This is called a system of checks and balances.

★ EXECUTIVE BRANCH

The executive branch enforces laws. It is made up of the president, the vice president, and the president's cabinet. The president represents the United States around the world. He or she oversees relations with other countries and signs treaties. The president signs bills into law and appoints officials and federal judges. He or she also leads the military and manages government workers.

★ LEGISLATIVE BRANCH

The legislative branch makes laws, maintains the military, and regulates trade. It also has the power to declare war. This branch consists of the Senate and the House of Representatives. Together, these two houses make up Congress. Each state has two senators. A state's population determines the number of representatives it has.

★ JUDICIAL BRANCH

The judicial branch interprets laws. It consists of district courts, courts of appeals, and the Supreme Court. District courts try cases. If a person disagrees with a trial's outcome, he or she may appeal. If a court of appeals supports the ruling, a person may appeal to the Supreme Court. The Supreme Court also makes sure that laws follow the US Constitution.

THE PRESIDENT ★

★ QUALIFICATIONS FOR OFFICE

To be president, a person must meet three requirements. A candidate must be at least 35 years old and a natural-born US citizen. He or she must also have lived in the United States for at least 14 years.

★ ELECTORAL COLLEGE

The US presidential election is an indirect election. Voters from each state choose electors to represent them in the Electoral College. The number of electors from each state is based on the state's population. Each elector has one electoral vote. Electors are pledged to cast their vote for the candidate who receives the highest number of popular votes in their state. A candidate must receive the majority of Electoral College votes to win.

★ TERM OF OFFICE

Each president may be elected to two four-year terms. Sometimes, a president may only be elected once. This happens if he or she served more than two years of the previous president's term.

The presidential election is held on the Tuesday after the first Monday in November. The president is sworn in on January 20 of the following year. At that time, he or she takes the oath of office:

> *I do solemnly swear (or affirm) that I will faithfully execute the office of President of the United States, and will to the best of my ability, preserve, protect and defend the Constitution of the United States.*

★ LINE OF SUCCESSION ★

The Presidential Succession Act of 1947 defines who becomes president if the president cannot serve. The vice president is first in the line of succession. Next are the Speaker of the House and the President Pro Tempore of the Senate. If none of these individuals is able to serve, the office falls to the president's cabinet members. They would take office in the order in which each department was created:

Secretary of State

Secretary of the Treasury

Secretary of Defense

Attorney General

Secretary of the Interior

Secretary of Agriculture

Secretary of Commerce

Secretary of Labor

Secretary of Health and Human Services

Secretary of Housing and Urban Development

Secretary of Transportation

Secretary of Energy

Secretary of Education

Secretary of Veterans Affairs

Secretary of Homeland Security

While in office, the president receives a salary of $400,000 each year. He or she lives in the White House and has 24-hour Secret Service protection.

The president may travel on a Boeing 747 jet called Air Force One. The airplane can accommodate 76 passengers. It has kitchens, a dining room, sleeping areas, and a conference room. It also has fully equipped offices with the latest communications systems. Air Force One can fly halfway around the world before needing to refuel. It can even refuel in flight!

Air Force One

If the president wishes to travel by car, he or she uses Cadillac One. It has been modified with heavy armor and communications systems. The president takes

Cadillac One

Cadillac One along when visiting other countries if secure transportation will be needed.

The president also travels on a helicopter called Marine One. Like the presidential car, Marine One accompanies the president when traveling abroad if necessary.

Sometimes, the president needs to get away and relax with family and friends. Camp David is the official presidential retreat. It is located in the cool, wooded mountains of Maryland. The US Navy maintains the retreat, and the US Marine Corps keeps it secure. The camp offers swimming, tennis, golf, and hiking.

When the president leaves office, he or she receives lifetime Secret Service protection. He or she also receives a yearly pension of $207,800 and funding for office space, supplies, and staff.

Marine One

George Washington

Abraham Lincoln

Theodore Roosevelt

	PRESIDENT	PARTY	TOOK OFFICE
1	George Washington	None	April 30, 1789
2	John Adams	Federalist	March 4, 1797
3	Thomas Jefferson	Democratic-Republican	March 4, 1801
4	James Madison	Democratic-Republican	March 4, 1809
5	James Monroe	Democratic-Republican	March 4, 1817
6	John Quincy Adams	Democratic-Republican	March 4, 1825
7	Andrew Jackson	Democrat	March 4, 1829
8	Martin Van Buren	Democrat	March 4, 1837
9	William H. Harrison	Whig	March 4, 1841
10	John Tyler	Whig	April 6, 1841
11	James K. Polk	Democrat	March 4, 1845
12	Zachary Taylor	Whig	March 5, 1849
13	Millard Fillmore	Whig	July 10, 1850
14	Franklin Pierce	Democrat	March 4, 1853
15	James Buchanan	Democrat	March 4, 1857
16	Abraham Lincoln	Republican	March 4, 1861
17	Andrew Johnson	Democrat	April 15, 1865
18	Ulysses S. Grant	Republican	March 4, 1869
19	Rutherford B. Hayes	Republican	March 3, 1877

THEIR TERMS ★

LEFT OFFICE	TERMS SERVED	VICE PRESIDENT
March 4, 1797	Two	John Adams
March 4, 1801	One	Thomas Jefferson
March 4, 1809	Two	Aaron Burr, George Clinton
March 4, 1817	Two	George Clinton, Elbridge Gerry
March 4, 1825	Two	Daniel D. Tompkins
March 4, 1829	One	John C. Calhoun
March 4, 1837	Two	John C. Calhoun, Martin Van Buren
March 4, 1841	One	Richard M. Johnson
April 4, 1841	Died During First Term	John Tyler
March 4, 1845	Completed Harrison's Term	Office Vacant
March 4, 1849	One	George M. Dallas
July 9, 1850	Died During First Term	Millard Fillmore
March 4, 1853	Completed Taylor's Term	Office Vacant
March 4, 1857	One	William R.D. King
March 4, 1861	One	John C. Breckinridge
April 15, 1865	Served One Term, Died During Second Term	Hannibal Hamlin, Andrew Johnson
March 4, 1869	Completed Lincoln's Second Term	Office Vacant
March 4, 1877	Two	Schuyler Colfax, Henry Wilson
March 4, 1881	One	William A. Wheeler

	PRESIDENT	PARTY	TOOK OFFICE
20	James A. Garfield	Republican	March 4, 1881
21	Chester Arthur	Republican	September 20, 1881
22	Grover Cleveland	Democrat	March 4, 1885
23	Benjamin Harrison	Republican	March 4, 1889
24	Grover Cleveland	Democrat	March 4, 1893
25	William McKinley	Republican	March 4, 1897
26	Theodore Roosevelt	Republican	September 14, 1901
27	William Taft	Republican	March 4, 1909
28	Woodrow Wilson	Democrat	March 4, 1913
29	Warren G. Harding	Republican	March 4, 1921
30	Calvin Coolidge	Republican	August 3, 1923
31	Herbert Hoover	Republican	March 4, 1929
32	Franklin D. Roosevelt	Democrat	March 4, 1933
33	Harry S. Truman	Democrat	April 12, 1945
34	Dwight D. Eisenhower	Republican	January 20, 1953
35	John F. Kennedy	Democrat	January 20, 1961

Franklin D. Roosevelt

John F. Kennedy

Ronald Reagan

LEFT OFFICE	TERMS SERVED	VICE PRESIDENT
September 19, 1881	Died During First Term	Chester Arthur
March 4, 1885	Completed Garfield's Term	Office Vacant
March 4, 1889	One	Thomas A. Hendricks
March 4, 1893	One	Levi P. Morton
March 4, 1897	One	Adlai E. Stevenson
September 14, 1901	Served One Term, Died During Second Term	Garret A. Hobart, Theodore Roosevelt
March 4, 1909	Completed McKinley's Second Term, Served One Term	Office Vacant, Charles Fairbanks
March 4, 1913	One	James S. Sherman
March 4, 1921	Two	Thomas R. Marshall
August 2, 1923	Died During First Term	Calvin Coolidge
March 4, 1929	Completed Harding's Term, Served One Term	Office Vacant, Charles Dawes
March 4, 1933	One	Charles Curtis
April 12, 1945	Served Three Terms, Died During Fourth Term	John Nance Garner, Henry A. Wallace, Harry S. Truman
January 20, 1953	Completed Roosevelt's Fourth Term, Served One Term	Office Vacant, Alben Barkley
January 20, 1961	Two	Richard Nixon
November 22, 1963	Died During First Term	Lyndon B. Johnson

	PRESIDENT	PARTY	TOOK OFFICE
36	Lyndon B. Johnson	Democrat	November 22, 1963
37	Richard Nixon	Republican	January 20, 1969
38	Gerald Ford	Republican	August 9, 1974
39	Jimmy Carter	Democrat	January 20, 1977
40	Ronald Reagan	Republican	January 20, 1981
41	George H.W. Bush	Republican	January 20, 1989
42	Bill Clinton	Democrat	January 20, 1993
43	George W. Bush	Republican	January 20, 2001
44	Barack Obama	Democrat	January 20, 2009
45	Donald Trump	Republican	January 20, 2017

Barack Obama

★ PRESIDENTS MATH GAME ★

Have fun with this presidents math game! First, study the list above and memorize each president's name and number. Then, use math to figure out which president completes each equation below.

1. Barack Obama – Jimmy Carter = ?

2. Jimmy Carter – Andrew Johnson = ?

3. Jimmy Carter + Thomas Jefferson = ?

Answers: 1. James Monroe ($44 - 39 = 5$)
2. Grover Cleveland ($39 - 17 = 22$)
3. Bill Clinton ($39 + 3 = 42$)